ISAAC NOWELL was bor   o
town of Newlyn in Cornwall. He read English
Literature at Balliol College, Oxford and com-
pleted his masters on twentieth-century literature
at the University of St Andrews. His work has
been published in the *TLS*, *Los Angeles Review of
Books*, *Lighthouse*, and *Pain*. He currently works
as a fisherman and is completing his first novella.
The Fountain is his debut collection of poems.

The Fountain

—

ISAAC NOWELL

—

ꟼP

PARTUS

OXFORD · REYKJAVÍK

MMXX

The Fountain

© Isaac Nowell, 2020

First published in Great Britain in 2020 by Partus Press Ltd.

266 Banbury Road, Oxford OX2 7DL

www.partus.press

A CIP catalogue record for this book is available from the

British Library, ISBN 9781913196028

The right of Isaac Nowell to be identified as the author of

this work has been asserted in accordance with the Copyright,

Designs and Patents Act of 1988. All rights reserved.

Designed in Oxford by Studio Lamont.

Printed and bound in Estonia.

THE FOUNTAIN

'I'll let you be in my dream if I can be in your dream.'

BOB DYLAN

When we were under Vienna: the dark
and lack, and white lights fading, coming back
and showing only wrecks of persons, things.
Scarred riverbeds and dead pistachio trees
locked up in January. This
and that I can't remember (persons, things).
In a shuttered flat above a shop, I know
I cry for the dead things unknowingly.
My dull god watches me and laughs and laughs
and laughs and watches laughing, cooing
I love you with the love of failed desire;
that is: in debt, reproach; that is: I don't.

Birds scattered like the wasting of a dream
to where El Greco's Christ's eyes pointed
and suddenly the fingers felt
their fragile journeying. I took them then
and hid them from your gaze, ashamed
of all they couldn't say. The eyes
I felt along my ribs. Was I asleep
like a black rabbit? Locking the door,
you laughed. I picked a pilchard's spine, convinced
that it, or such a one, would play a part
in my own death. Whichever way was left
burst its hold, and the sun on us.

Wind whistled in the window and the door
shook on its hinges, and you looked to me
a young John Baptist *del passeggio*
(uncanny, so I thought), and so I caught,
to gather up the moment in my hands,
your hands, and brought them to my lips and blew
(your cupped hands cupped in mine like blighted petals
blown). Dust swam up fluorescently
away from languages of use and ice,
and when the stillness came and we went out
there was no colour in the city, but
three birds rose from a burning orange tree.

Rain silvered distant traffic, conjured with
a quick grim stare. A piece of paper bore
the news of death (your death) and gryllos
leaned torsioned out in carnival delight.
There was no want of comic timing. PAUSE
FOR LAUGHTER. Hesitatingly withdrew,
the man, a can of Special Brew, and sipp't
as if to manifest his loss...
The bus persisted through a series of
damp paper villages. On the horizon
rigs sat watchful. The man to himself
said, *my friend, we are not free not to look.*

The anger that united us divided
us also. So much was unsurprising
when the sun gave up, and the white lights burned
like snow on glass on skin. The flood
of events stammered, truncated again,
bankrupted again. We saw her curled
foetal, abortive in the road. Blindness
presumed as much of us, although
some sounds, some limbs, are since recorded:
observe the leg crook'd up to meet the brow,
the other jackknifed there below;
a hand (your hand) bit back like boiling oil.

As now you turn your back to fountain, trees
(whereat the dust is gone) shining,
and I do not know if I am dreaming,
and your eyes have places that I cannot go
that look like when the rain came falling,
and we were young and let it come, and you
still turning now from fountain,
and trees now shining strongly on your hands
unquestioning that take my hands
into them independent of delight and
sadness. You give me from them not sadness
really, or love, but overwhelming need of sleep.

Two men moved arguing on wheels that would
revolve a stand of postcards out
of shot. The motions retrograde. The gift-
shop lit with votive candles gloamed full-smooth,
threw smoke and incense out into the street
where air was sweet with nascent rain. Consumed
anticipation bordered halflight coolly,
hugged to cement stone plastic cheap alloy-
compounds, all in a foil of rain beginning.
The footsteps echoed out of reach of light,
which is to say: without a way demarked
in floodlit darkness voices peter out.

The moon: a bitten bit of thumbnail spat
at gritted streets. Where else lacunae but
the moon's? Kept coming, sweetly
bivouacking us. With unquiet eyes the stilled,
entrenched, melodious farce you brushed away
was born again, and died (again born, dead).
What else were faces but the long way back?
Future subsists so eloquently, grand-
iloquently. Lungs hollowed out of air.
Again the corpse sunk in the fountain rose
and offered us directions to the party
with aid of flavourful gesticulation.

A boy looks up from where he stands, from where
he waits for what he doesn't understand,
as birds wake up before the dawn, the rain,
and light returns to what remains. It shows
a man go slowly from his sleep with hands
to bruiséd eyes and rising leave the room.
The boy looks down the road, and up, and twice.
The rain comes heavy down. He turns his head
to see the face appear below. The lights
come on. Two bowls laid out in little light. Unend
of motion owning pain.
The man sits heavy down. He waits again.

She said, this is the edge of the darkness,
describing with a soft pale arc the place
a fox shot from a hedgerow, flickered weightless,
a failing headlight burst. All this at once.
Insomniac with soured cream, so much
is unsurprising in the city where
the soporific air is thick with sweet
fluorescent lights that burn all night and light
the dark way back to a choked fountain's lip.
Or so the chant enchanted: our delight
in spite objectifying time gone lately,
and time gone lately lapping at your step.

Your smile etiolated in the carpark.
With slender skill the barman drew it back.
Munchausenly tall, O my dear Alphonse,
my metic, was the Great Thaw coming, slugly
up waterbreak? St Stephen cloaked in scaffolding
and stars out were a kind of joke, like
the obstinate lacuna of sense,
laceratingly renewed, when the gentle
sad beauty of your ear, you said, was one
way of becoming absenter. The beer
did not become you, and we were becoming
lost (in terms of knowing where we were).

It was the era of the adverb, the
verb being cauterised. And all at once
the fingers felt their fragile bludgeoning.
A mouth, like slack elastic, puckered up,
misrecognising us. Your countenance
of cold appraisal then. *Until when will
you not be quiet?* We met one from the suburbs
(sixties-blossomed) elucidating why
there was a room above the room above
the room above the room that was the sky.
She said the fear she'd had before that she
had never owned died with her mother's death.

For instance overwhelmed because the odds,
at times impossible to comprehend,
become an act of abnegation and
as now the two men hung there twist
and drift from side to side the question is
less how they came to be the ones who twist
and drift from side to side in supple breezes,
their heads snapped back like dustbin lids, but more
with all the ways Atropos comes, why this?
Which is to say, with all
the ways to cease existence, why
the evolution of the noose, whose odds must be?

The sun divided rubble, quietly
absurd because it could. I thought you would
be silenter with a bust back, the world
be flatter than we'd asked, and death.
Expiring of so rare an illness was
already cause for self-congratulation.
If only I were present at my own
dissection: pleasures of hydratic and
polyous matter, with roots in the bronchi
and branches reaching as far as the larynx!
She'd come to me back then no less than twenty
times daily, asking for chocolate, lemonade.

Obfuscator, whose limbs dismantle,
the fountain closing round us steadily,
(and whether memory or bricolage
I can't decide (you say you thought
the dead were buried under us and not))
gives up a sigh that settles as the arm
describes a gentle arc as darkness falling,
fallen, softens the edges of the forms,
as birds' wings settle back to hide a face,
to come back slowly: had to, slowly: had to.
I drank for two weeks when Napoleon died.
A towel is being tautened in my head.

Come little iconoclast smelling of love,
one thumbnail split and a big mouth hung
like her with the closed eyes drifting supine,
tugged by the tide's pull, reeking sweetly
of alcohol sweetly and sick and sweat
and love. Prosopopeia, so far, I
am sorry, purblind, and forgetful. TO
ma funky LADIES: *je n'ai plus de feu!* –
my dull god watches me, a countenance
of cold appraisal truly from the wall
whose hairline crack runs down my back like sweat
with sweat that mingles with your sweat and pools.

The next night's mistake was when I was taken
to be a bullfighter by one of Hollywood's
brightest stars. I ventured that
we were too too late. The headless giant
Orion expostulated wildly on
the telly, was incipient. It seemed
to me to be ridonkulous, a *mise
en abîme,* forever efflorescent.
Aporias of time soiled the carpet,
red like the bloods of strangers, you observed,
the scene still closing round us like a lily
and waves kept coming that keep coming that

Turns out I'm having dreams again
of tenderness that shake me as I miss
the big sad eyes I've never seen, and trace
the shoulder's skin along and wake
all wet with tears. Poetry first, sausage
later. Realising also my hands
refused (or were unable) to move
you took them to you safely, then away
and brought me on a tray some lemonade,
a soft-boiled egg, and something colourless
(a city) I couldn't identify.
The rain continued to fall in your absence.

A thousand chickens' eggs were hatching in
slow motion sepia, and Wien bestirred.
I smashed my glass exquisitely, besides,
to watch the glass in slow motion also
itself release from form. Were many souls set free
in this and other ways? Were many blistered?
He had a gentle neck and heavy eyes
that lingered as the lights went out all over.
My lungs (or is it my heart?) are failing,
probably there's not much here of worth:
some other animals I love, of which,
some me, some things some others oneday made.

The light relinquishing the empire, or
the empire light, down Linzer Straße
lazily smiled the dogman. Nightwalking
and daywalking distinguishable only
in name, he spun his supple cane and shone
his teeth, was gratified, was satisfied
one noonday gone. And all beneath the sun
and other ways, and other ones, there were
they say, alive to this day, for all time,
the sins of the delicatessen
known often by the fountain when the moon
comes creeping low across the stone.

An one who partook hugely of celery
midsentence turned – the rough music ringing –
to rip the room roundly, and me. So far
so good, he said with a look, and by hook
or by crook (for he *was* a grand larcen)
he whet upon the party savagely
his wit. Was tipex'd on the windowpane
the cold command *leave me alone.* At last
I could begin to understand, observe
the burden of the herbivore across
the folding table, wrinkled lightly there
and there, and there again along the torn linoleum.

A pile of bones – some skulls, the bigger ones –
lay in a ring just off the road that led
up to the path that hid itself in cloud
which when we left the circle of burnt bones
we followed hard across the knotted heather
(falling down often to the heather)
where shattered granite often
lay taut like a waiting animal
and when the wind awoke and held our hair
its icy fingers whispered all our names
and then we broke the reach of cloud and were
thrown on our backs by rivers of red deer.

So far it is clear I have failed to tell you
what I have failed to understand, and failing
fallen from outer banks of reason, blue
escarpments in a sallow season, burning
where last distractions are discovered trailing
blindly onto sickly waters, where
the warm flies bruise the air and come and go
and kiss my skin with whispers of despair,
and draw the blood from me, which goes like snow
like smoke away, just like the ballast has
itself absolved, perhaps dissolved, perhaps
not dissolved. Perhaps the burden of it lasts.

Bent on the steps of Greenwich Naval College,
whose name I didn't know, halfdrunk at eight,
plumb out of love I fell. I tried to say
the quiet tragedy of failing love
is on the gentle air of London Town
but thought how stupid that would sound,
with morning's dull ache waiting
inarticulate for me, and you. I fled
to dolphins in the centre spitting water
to seek their staunch advice, but all they said
were things I couldn't hear. I was
surprised, them looking wise, but also they *were* stones.

I slept our twenty years away and dreamed
knuckles shuttering eyes. Had there been some
insane mistake? You came back faceless. There is
no subtlety to this. There stoop the men
and the women young with grey hair, with
only their bodies' forms betraying youth,
and doors are shut against us. They beat, too,
at doors wearily, exhaling moth-
born particles of dust that gutter in
the sunken coils of moonlight and ignite…
Your smell was on me for a week until
it wasted in May like a gentle thing.

In spring the dawn in summer night in autumn
evening in winter the early morning
in spring the dawn in summer night in autumn
evening in winter the early morning
in spring the dawn in summer night in autumn
evening in winter the early morning
in spring the dawn in summer night in autumn
evening in winter the early morning
in spring the dawn in summer night in autumn
evening in winter the early morning
in spring the dawn in summer night in autumn
evening in winter the early morning

A bead of sweat described a world, or something out of mind defined. With all of this
(pubescence and the bloated dark) enclosing
like steel bars on our ears,
the twisting and the loosened lips
unwound without closure; the conversation
of bodies (heavenly or otherwise)
declined through lesions of misrule (subtle
refinements of subtleties misremembered).
You slewed into the snow in gentle bows
of urine the word *resurgam*. You I
loved, and the shadows of falling snow on snow.

More than the story of my own insolvent
tottering onwards (someone was talking) I
am torqued by the tongue of Creusa. *Venez-*
vous m'enlever dans l'éternelle nuit?
And who's this walking my way now
across the wild field like a dead one?
And how shall I ever forgive him this:
his coming to destroy my beauty?
With his looks of a madman brandishing
a razor glinting in the sun, I see
he'll come to me always, forever, wishing
to free my golden hair and make me free.

Somewhere behind another faintly raised
a blue hand to his eyes, and said, *My thoughts
are not your thoughts*, and tears came to his eyes,
and darkness clotted into birds and shook,
and settled like the dust along his lids,
and the fountain stuttered to life and shot
a flute of rusted water through the dark,
by no means prematurely. The late snow
in April when the moon was on us fell
like someone's dream. There were no clouds to see.
There were no clouds discernible. There are
no clouds to see at all. Of this I'm sure.

With anger misdirected or without
a proper object, come to me at night:
with one big beery paunch, a humping grudge
and ill-defined profusions of your rights,
come strongly to me in the night, or with
the corner of your left eye bloodied come.
Come sing to me the lies that I can love.
I'll see your eyes are lit within by something bruising and coagulate. I'll shake
your hand still torn and muddied at the tips,
and watch your lips begin to move the silence.
And there's not much more I can take of this.

Rain falls again. Birds move. The sun is on them
sometimes. Concerning what is masticated:
go south the birds, ourselves. The people come
and look like empty cans, and one
bent to a gravestone finds the words have left
marks of pain alone. In between the wind,
the sounds of voices. There are things we can
afford: the things we can afford. Too small
a time for that. Forgiveness stretches only
as such. *Shut up*, you say, when I am doleful.
And I think of your ridiculous beauty.
By this beauty (briefly) I am amazed.

Nobody say, *the fountain*! Is there some
fun in keeping the noun from others? Is
the hollow sound of a tapped sternum one
of many kinds of joke? Failure another.
I wonder how much pressure to fracture
a jawbone would be needed. I concede
no expertise in likes of this. I see
the pain of the faces holds the plateau
above the heads that holds above the heads
a man, a woman, and a child. TO GO
THE DISTANCE! Such a flaw in the indenture
as seems to be concerning us, remove.

Much like the evolution of the noose,
your face. Much like the dolour of the rose,
deface the low gate slowly swinging closed.
Much like the failure you have sensed return
as sunlight breaks the blinds to burn your eyes
as moonlight breaks the blinds to burn your eyes
where is the world we are dismembering?
where is the shallow hiss of cuttlefish
or cuttlebone along the lonely sand –
writes ribbons of such learned discerning verse(!),
which pricks your forehead later as the moon
is beating at the blinds to burn your eyes?

Not understanding that which I had failed
to believe, but believing in the failure,
I asked the doctor for a cup of water,
and rose without pain to the plastic lip
she offered while the yellow light glid softly
on tubes and machinery. The noise
of it all was a lot of noise. And then
there were the thoughts of how I came to be here,
where nothing can persuade my hands to move,
as if it will be so forever.
In the room there is a child that moans at night.
I think perhaps it means it is afraid.

How can I say that all the thankless acts,
of which I can remember none, reduce
me now to tears, which gather in my hands?
How can I say that when you came to me
I did not think, but understood how love
in detail could contour the earth, own certain
seconds? That I saw the blood also scarring
the earth, and I felt it to be the only
answer to your question? How can I say
each kindness was a kind of retrospective
violence, however slight, done in light
of all the things that I had done to you?

When later we arrived and went below,
where bodies turned in darkness, torsioned out
in carnival delight, the light broke down
the faces intermittently that rose
from out of darkness laughing madly with
their rolling eyes they couldn't still,
and all the world was one big wonderful
dangerous accident. Purveyed a sense
of opportunity. I felt myself
dissolving as the lights dissolved my features
and hid them in the darkened corners, where
they met with others of that vacancy.

In consequence the wound was harmless, and
Winnie the Pooh loomed large in my conscience
with a barrel of honey not even
he was able to finish, with Piglet,
with raised voices, and with voices whose panic
I could feel like the waiting for the Mobile
Retail Service (MRS) to arrive...
The train feigned stillness till the stillness gave
on what seemed so delectable. The thoughts
of Pooh were neither here nor there: too soon
I would be met with a dear face. I would
do what I could to stop the tears from coming.

Considered holding in my hands your two
benippled breasts. Expect I'd go beyond
the reach of consciousness, and wake years later
in a strange world peopled chiefly by squirrels,
a mustachioed gentleman over me,
with hat of fantastic plumage, pulling
gently on the larger of my testicles,
that is, on the left of my testicles
(ringstraked speckled and grisled). In the mizzle
I'd see what had become of humankind
and, unsurprised, relinquish any claims
of superiority over squirrels.

For the unlikelihood of finding a corpse
while walking in the woods (it happened once,
unwelcome intrusion) I'm truly grateful.
The laughter is sometimes inopportune.
Perhaps because of what has taken place
of silence. Perhaps because of the boredom.
Certainly sparrows glint and dart in suburbs.
Certainly we have too much privilege
to choose from. Certainly the sun
was on his neck and back, besides
the buzzards forming like some torn-up shadow.
There is nothing beautiful about death.

Forfend the self-disgust, if possible;
chemically provoke sensations of
determination in the hopeless. Go
the way of the late, great Uriah Heep.
Descend and weep. Betray the accidental
moments of candour, blundering, lightly,
as if delighted. O if, obsolescent
summoner, ever you come to me, will
you bring me Diet Coke and dirty chips
aplenty to consume? We can consume
the products that you bring to us as if
they were the fluttering of little souls.

O delicate attenuator, when
will all of it be over? Am I just
a vehicle by which my death is living?
I found this one asleep between two hanged men.
The ring finger of his right hand was crippled,
tented at the second knuckle.
It's clear: a vast speculation has failed.
Do you see how the drunk moon holds me,
and the pain crawls round inside my head
from side to side, and side to side, and back?
how in the end it's dark and lack,
and what we used to think were things we were?

Yes, obstreperous cantatrice, will you
replace my worsted hands and eyes? I know
how you have gone with them away from me.
It's true, in moments of weakness, I wonder
if you have gone away with love, but true
when morning comes (is coming early now)
I know what my delusions are. I see
you are the cat that got the cream, you are
a hundred thousand singularities.
With all your darkened ways, please come to me,
beringed and jewel-behung (upholstered), come –
come bravely to me at the witching hour.

Devoured by your illness in the winter,
you came to me in spring, again. I knew
you by the web of blood about your mouth,
the blackened rings around your eyes.
You kissed my cheek and led me by the hand
to that sweeter place, with the orange fish.
I wondered at your silence and was sad
and hung my head. You took a cigarette,
rolled long ago, and lit the tip, and drew
the smoke in deeply. And I couldn't go.
You held my hands, my eyes, said nothing still
and I was sad for it, and glad as well.

His lips peeled back in death, his poor distended
belly was more than I could bear. The fare
was reasonable, however. The clear
day beat the roadside, passionless. In time
I would forget my weakness. Stars
grew stronger in the softness of the air.
How then to reconcile these thoughts with thoughts
of everything that came before? Again,
he's in the hedgerow, in the crippled sedge,
an empty bottle tight against his chest,
lips parted, eyes closed, quieted. He does
and doesn't smile. All the green sky is dying.

A plane crawls past the moon. Like something seeking
its own extinction. All that happens is
the place seems like a place I've seen; the face
like distant music, half-imagined, gives
reason to this, and alters nothing. Air
grown thick with summer remembers all over
how rain surprised us on our journey, falling
on hands, in eyes, like each one's compulsion
to speak of suffering when it is silent.
Birds move across the moon. Who is it moves
along the path before me (pathway roofed
with hawthorn) glimpsed at corners? No one now.

I wondered how the corrugated iron
had turned up in the hedgerow with a crisp-
packet and twenty disinfectant bottles
(discarded sediment of time), but they
were also touched by hands. Perhaps a man,
or woman with a friend, came here at night
and furtively absolved themselves each small
transgression as enacting it. But then,
perhaps they wept, and ate their own tears, weeping
all through it, and each motion of each hand
and eye was an agony suffered with
the set grim face of one that's lately dead.

Your eyes were soft with sorrow and moonlight
in a cavernous room. Each day we came
we came for this: to say we came
for this: to know you. Who was it beneath
the water of the fountain, looking up
forever at the sky? Put, I pray thee,
thy hand under my thigh. My eyes are dim
yet warm, and kindnesses magnificent.
Since so long ago I have loved, since time
before. Embarrassed once, remember, by
a feline gaze, which came between us, or
before us, threatening to break the process.

A young man sang in a ravishing fashion
of sharp tears pricking in the vacant heat,
of someone breaking in an empty station,
of what the world had taken back.
From out of each one swollen like a cancer
coming was always Future, out of each
the hunger and the anger and *will't please*
you eat? Will't please your highness feed? The light
pours down on centre stage, on thrust and rake,
proscenium arch and all the clever flesh
that's requisite to frame a night. I have
sought a gentler means of persuasion.

The horse cemetery, *le cimetière*
cheval, is on the corner, where the cure
for death is incineration, a cure
incidentally also for life.
Winter is very long. The hawthorn like
a bad coiffure: parting without being
forced. The offices
that profit us make jetsam of the human
and gather all the juicy bits and press
the hunger of the little mirror where
the lovely darkness raining from the trees
consumes the ludic twilight with a lisp.

Love is to do with the buck of your top
left lateral incisor. It is not
a delicacy I have tasted. There
is somewhere people waste apart from this,
or worse, and changing place is best,
and all of all the faces are distressed.
Dresse and undresse thy soul: mark the decay,
the total desolation of nostalgia
like laughter in the silence of the pine trees,
sirens beyond the stars heard, screeching as
I ask if he will take me to the place
the silver-blue sardines are seen.

A one arranging pebbles like a fish
as if to photograph, as if they were
a life curated, laughed and shook her hair
and asked us for directions to the place
the latest suicide would be performed,
detailed and repeated from a million
screens, forever, all over the world.
We asked her name, were curious, but she,
already turning from us, said
I am the Duchess of Malfi still,
and went off clutching a bitten pear,
a ruined artichoke all full of earwigs.

Her shirt plumed like a plastic bag, her skin
translucent, and the blues of her tattoos
were fading in our eyes, moved by the river,
and moved unspeaking elsewhere. In the night
I dreamt of striding across fields
of asphodel, while the cries of the dead
rang out like the birds' cries, and she related
my griefs to me as if they were a stranger's.
Can you see the Pripyat Ferris Wheel
from the sleek smooth glass gymnasium?
Two rooks entice a buzzard over alders.
And still there are the things I cannot say.

I found myself in a bare field, again
in the dread centre, again in a bare field
whose borders were beyond what I could see,
beneath a telegraph post with no wires,
on which a blackbird landed softly,
and looked around. The bird's eyes
were more intelligent than any eyes
I'd ever seen, and he stopped by
the silence patiently, as if it were
the child of an unloved acquaintance, loosed
a cry that made all my body shake
for several minutes, perhaps ten minutes.

By now we were returning to the place
which we had left in autumn, which of course
no longer existed, changed by rain.